Spring Harvest
Bible Wo

G000147174

Praying to an
Unlimited God in
Unlimited Ways

Prayer

First published in 2019 by Essential Christian
14 Horsted Square, Uckfield, TN22 1QG Tel: 01825 746530
Email: info@essentialchristian.org   Web: essentialchristian.org
Registered charity number 1126997

The rights of Paul & Paula Weston to be identified as authors
have been asserted by them in accordance with the Copyright,
Designs and Patents Act 1988.

*All rights reserved. No part of this publication may be reproduced, shared
in a retrieval system, or transmitted in any form or by any means, electronic,
mechanical, photocopying, recording or otherwise, without the prior
permission of the publisher or a licence permitting restricted copying.
In the UK such licences are issued by the Copyright Licensing Agency,
90 Tottenham Court Road, London W1P 9HE.*

British Library Cataloguing in Publication Data

All Scripture quotations unless indicated otherwise are taken from
THE HOLY BIBLE, NEW INTERNATIONAL VERSION, NIV
Copyright © 1973, 1978, 1984, 2011 by Biblica, Inc. Used by permission.
All rights reserved worldwide.

THE MESSAGE
Copyright © by Eugene H Peterson 1993, 1994, 1995, 1996, 2000, 2001, 2002.
Used by permission of NavPress. All rights reserved.
Represented by Tyndale House Publishers Inc.

A catalogue record for this book is available from the British Library.

ISBN 9781911237136

Cover Design by Cover design by Sublime
wearesubmlime.com

Designed by Ascent Creative

Printed by Halcyon

Contents

About the authors

Paul and Paula lead New Generation Church in South London. They have both experienced the power of prayer first-hand.

Paula says, 'My mum is what you might call an intercessor. As a young pre-schooler I remember often being taken to her friend Pat's house for the day and they would spend the day praying! Thankfully Pat had a daughter so we amused ourselves while the mums sat in the kitchen and prayed. Whenever life took a downward turn my mum would call all six kids together to pray with her. She led us to make agreements as a family in the name of Jesus.

Those agreements led to my dad giving his life to Jesus, my brother's healing from a severe reaction to medication, my healing from migraines, provision when it was most needed, cars starting that had broken down, even washing machines starting to work just to name a few of the miracles we saw. In my teens my parents prayed to keep me on the straight and narrow (there were a few detours, all of which were ended abruptly). I believe it was Mum's prayers that saw many of my friends turn their lives around and follow Jesus. Yes, I prayed too in those formative years but it was my parents who modelled how.'

Paul was introduced to the power of prayer when he returned home from working away. He discovered that a pretty girl, Paula had been introduced to his friendship group and she was one of those 'Christians'. He decided to set her straight only to find that he was on the receiving end of the power of prayer.

Unbeknownst to Paul, Paula and her mum had committed to praying for the leaders of the group, Paul being one of them. At the pub one night, egged on by cynically laughing friends, he received prayer for his badly damaged knee. Shocked when it was completely healed, Paul handed his life over to Jesus. Shortly after, he and Paula began their journey in prayer together.

Paul says, 'After giving my life to Jesus, Paula and I made a list of all our friends and committed to pray for them. In a short space of time many gave their lives to Jesus and then committed to pray for the others. A small praying community was born.'

It wasn't long before the now hungry-for-God Paul was introduced to church leadership and, meeting others with the same DNA, strategic friendships were formed. Paul says, 'It was a privilege to be involved in the very beginning of the 24/7 Prayer Movement'. Over 25 years later, despite challenges and disappointments along the way, the adventure in prayer and its outworking continues.

Introduction

Prayer, talking, and having an honest, simple dialogue with God, Jesus or Holy Spirit, becomes a lifestyle. Talking things over with Jesus, our friend who will never let us down, - even though we often do him - is not only therapeutic but changes things for the better. As you work through this study guide, dare to open up your heart and allow Holy Spirit to be your comforter and guide.
As, through prayer, you grow your relationship with all three of members of the Godhead, you will find your heart is made whole and you become more aware of people around you who need your prayers. Get closer still and God will share his secrets with you, Holy Spirit will have fun with you, and you will find Jesus is the best friend you could ever have.

Maddy Carvosso

 The hinge of history is the bended knee.
Prayer changes the world.

Pete Greig

About this book

The primary purpose of this book is for small groups but it can also be useful for individuals who want to enhance their prayer life. The intention throughout this six-part study is to inspire new and creative ways of praying, encourage persistence through stories of answered prayers, offer hope for those who find their current prayer life stale or frustrating.

We have several sections within each session and they can be recognised by the following headings:

 Straight from the heart - Each session begins with a story. Feel free to share your own story or experience as it relates to the chapter.

 Connect - An ice breaker/starter activity; time for the group to connect together.

 Creating space - A chance to look together at the subject material.

 Eat it up - A time to discuss and digest what you have read and go deeper. This contains extra verses, an activity, or further questions. You might want to break the group down into groups of twos or threes to talk together.

 Give it up - Time to focus on God through different types of prayer.

 Empowered life - Further study that can be completed during the week.

 Over the edge - A challenge to put your learning into action during the week.

> *Prayer is the point at which my worrying, over thinking, analysing and negative thoughts stop and turn in to a conversation with a living God who listens and understands and responds. Sometimes a few minutes with God shifts me out of a place that hours thinking or conversation with others can't, and often I find myself with a very different perspective than my own, a Kingdom perspective.*

Mary Rouse

Straight from the heart

'I am a busy parent of three small children and it is not always possible for me to find time to sit quietly listening to God or spend lots of time praying through different things. I used to feel guilty about this, but I am learning that prayer can be a continual two-way conversation with God. I might not have time to sit and listen in silence to what he has to say to me, but I hear him in other ways - a breath of peace in the chaos of trying to get out of the house for the school run or a Bible verse that comes to mind as I push the buggy to the park. I don't often have time to sit and pray creatively or very thoughtfully, but I'm learning to pray using words from the Bible or songs, things that are swirling around my head. My prayers are often simple and quick, "Lord, I'm tired this morning," and I know that his answer is, 'My strength is enough for you, my power is made perfect in weakness.' I am reliant on truths that are in my heart and I am learning to recognise his still, small voice in the middle of my busyness, as my life becomes less a series of dedicated prayer times and more a long conversation with Jesus that brings with it a sense of friendship and love that I carry through each day.

Clare Stevens

Read the passage:

The Lord's Prayer

This, then, is how you should pray:

'Our Father in heaven, hallowed be your name,
your kingdom come, your will be done,
On earth as it is in heaven.
Give us today our daily bread.
And forgive us our debts, as we also have forgiven our debtors.
And lead us not into temptation, but deliver us from the evil one'

Matthew 6:9-13

 # Connect

Play 'How's yours?'

You will require a group of people to team up against one guesser. Team members decide on an object that should be fairly common and something everybody would have such as a passport, a mobile phone or an email account. It's a bit like Twenty Questions, but the only question the guesser is allowed to ask is 'How's yours?' If you only have a few people the guesser will ask individuals more than once but must question each person in turn, 'How's yours?'

The questioned individual then provides an honest clue (not too easy and not too hard) that will help the guesser figure out the object. The guesser is entitled to only one guess per clue. If the guesser is able to correctly answer from your clue, then you have to be the next guesser.

 It never ceases to amaze me, that we – formerly unlovely, sexually unclean, self-centred, dishonest, opinionated and arrogant – should, through Christ's death and resurrection, be invited to the purity and honesty of Heaven – and engage in conversations and requests to our Creator Saviour and get responses, endorsements and miracles. What an incredible journey, from darkness to light!

Gerald Coates

 # Creating space

My thoughts and notes...

What is prayer?

Prayer is the conversations, the interactions and the communications you have with your father in heaven.

We are all unique in the way we communicate. Our conversations may take place through twitter, email or mobile phone, just to name a few mediums through which we talk to each other. Forms of communication have changed over centuries and we no longer use smoke signals, trumpet calls or town criers. But one thing that hasn't changed since the beginning, is our ability to pray and have a hotline direct to our creator.

Prayer is not only communication and where we grow relationship with God, but it's a generator of the power of God that will change lives, cities and nations. Prayer is not just words, it's not just Bible study, it is a lifestyle.

Although there is no set formula for how and when we should pray, the Bible gives us helpful guidelines.

The Lord's Prayer is a great starting point:

Spend some time thinking about the different aspects of the Lord's Prayer and the journey it takes you on.

Our Father in heaven, hallowed be your name.

We start by acknowledging who we are talking to: the God who created the universe, the one true God who is also our Father. He's a good father who deserves our respect and a loving father who holds us close. Prayer is a chance for us to show our love for him and to be thankful for who he is: holy, worthy, before all things, above all things, the creator and giver of life.

Your kingdom come.

God's kingdom is a place where he reigns - in our lives and our circumstances. The kingdom can be released around us. Acknowledge who God is, your dependence on him as a loving father, but also as a ruler on a heavenly throne. You're allowed to ask the king!

Your will be done, on earth as it is in heaven.

We should be asking for God's will, not our own, to be done in our lives. We can ask for all that God has in heaven for us and those around us to be released here on earth. Imagine what heaven is like: no sickness, no pain, no lack, no disconnection from our father.

Give us today our daily bread.

God wants to supply our every need. He will look after his children. He has what we need, emotionally, mentally and physically. There is no lack in his provision for us.

And forgive us our debts, as we also have forgiven our debtors.

We can confidently ask for forgiveness for anything we have done wrong; for any offence, for unforgiveness, for not trusting God or holding onto disappointment. Then because of God's forgiveness extended to us we can forgive others.

And lead us not into temptation,

We can ask God to help us recognise any trap of the enemy, and then we must flee from any temptations put in our path and stay focused on God's truth, plan and promises.

But deliver us from the evil one.

The enemy's plans are often subtle and as we spend time before God and in his presence we can ask him to search our hearts and know us and know any anxious thoughts in us. As Psalm 91 reminds us, God is our deliverer.

Prayer grows our relationship with God.

Just as in any relationship, we grow closer to God as we spend time together and communicate.

When we begin any relationship, communication styles are learnt and adapted. In teams or in a marriage we might choose to invest in evaluating and developing our communication preferences, personality types or love languages. However, it's only as we begin the journey of relationship that we learn how to effectively and intimately communicate.

There is no need to talk to God with religious language or change your tone of voice or kneel (but of course you may want to express your emotions in different ways). We can talk to him as we talk to a best friend. We can be completely vulnerable with our weaknesses; we can trust wholeheartedly that he loves us just as we are. In the Old Testament there was some cleaning up that had to happen before people approached God, but we can come as we are and know that Jesus has made us clean.

My thoughts and notes...

> *Prayer is becoming a place of contact where I trade my list for Jesus' list - they are rarely the same.*
>
> *Prayer in private trains me to hear in public.*
>
> Chris Abbington

 # Eat it up

Talk together about your rhythm of prayer. Maybe some of you find getting up early to pray works best but others find it easier to pray during the day or in the evening. Some might pray while running or driving and others prefer to be still and quiet.

A child often only communicates needs to their parent: "can I have....", "I am hungry", "I am thirsty." But as they mature and grow the relationship changes and they have more two-way conversations, talking about life together and not just communicating needs.

As a parent of teens I have not stopped meeting my children's needs or caring whether they have what they need. Likewise, they still let me know their needs but there is more dialogue about concerns, achievements, fears, joys, friendships and ideas. I think it is the same in our prayer life with our heavenly father. God will always be interested in meeting our needs, but our prayer life becomes much more than a list of asks as our relationship with God matures.

What's exciting about this relationship is that we are not expected to learn alone; we have God's Holy Spirit as our helper and counsellor. God doesn't just want us to read his word; he wants us to hear him speaking today too. He also wants us to experience his presence. We do this through the Holy Spirit.

We may communicate with many of our friends through social media but nothing can substitute being with friends physically. God, the maker of the universe, wants to come close. Jesus made a way for us to step right into God's presence, so prayer may start off with words but it's so much more than that.

Talk about ways you have experienced God's presence.

Maybe there was a time you were fearful and you suddenly felt calm or peaceful. Perhaps you began to feel repentant, happy, tearful or joyful. Maybe you saw a vision in your mind's eye or you had new inspiration.

The Bible talks a lot about coming into God's presence with thanksgiving. When we start our conversation with God by giving thanks to him, we open the gates into his inner sanctuary.

Jesus is the way, the truth and the life. He is the way to the father. Through the death and resurrection of Jesus we can enter into God's sanctuary.

It used to be just the priests who could enter into the Holy of Holies but now we are the priesthood. We are sons and daughters. Be expectant as you enter his presence and begin to commune with him.

Look together at James 5:16, *'The prayer of a righteous person is powerful and effective.'* (NIV)

How have you experienced the power of God through prayer?

Give it up

Depending on the number of people in your group, you may want to split into smaller groups for this exercise. People often find it easier to express themselves in smaller groups.

Each group will need pen and paper and a Bible. Come back together for feedback at the end. Ask if anyone was surprised by the verses they read, or if anyone has a problem believing God would want to do what the verses talk about for them. Sometimes if people lack confidence in themselves and how God sees them they find it easy to believe other people can ask God for things, or that God would want to provide for others but not for them. But God's promises are for all his children.

Have you noticed how generous our father God is? He has so much he wants to give to us, his children.

Take some time to write down some of the things he wants to give you:

John 16:13

2 Thessalonians 2:16-17

1 John 1:2

2 Corinthians 1:3-4

Romans 15:13

2 Thessalonians 3:3

2 Timothy 3:16

Hebrews 4:16

We don't spend time with God because we have to but because we want to. We are not slaves or sinners but sons and daughters. Yes, just like going to the gym, prayer takes discipline and there is sometimes a resistance in our natural bodies to do it, but we don't pray to justify ourselves or to prove ourselves to God. In fact, prayer requires humility.

Give us this day our daily bread.

1. Put aside any false beliefs that God does not want to give good things to you (for some people this will be an ongoing process and one they may need help with).

2. Ask him to provide for your:

   a. Physical needs - strength, food, health, warmth, finance

   b. Emotional needs- joy, security in God's love, peace, sound mind

   c. Spiritual needs - knowing his love and presence, greater sensitivity to the Holy Spirit, our helper and counsellor.

Having looked at the preceding passages, what does God want to say to you about your personal needs and the needs of those around you?

Take some time to write down what you hear.

Empowered life

> **❝** *I am persuaded that if a Christian who has understood the need to pray but does not pray they will backslide.* **❞**
>
> John Wesley

If you are a believer you have been called to pray.

- 'Much praying is not done because we do not plan to pray. We do not drift into spiritual life; we do not drift into disciplined prayer.' (D A Carson)

- We will not grow in prayer unless we plan to pray. That means we must deliberately set aside time to pray.

- Prayer is us learning to express trust in God and it is where our faith and trust in our heavenly father can increase.

- Prayer is communion and fellowship with God. Prayer is a two-way conversation. God wants to talk to you too.

- Prayer enters you into an intimate relationship with God. He is a good father.

Balanced prayer embraces worship and thanksgiving to God and intercession for others as well as our own personal petitions.

The foundation of our prayers must be the word of God, the Bible. As we hear the word and believe the word of God our faith grows and matures.

I wonder how many times I have thought I'd love to spend some time in prayer but I'm just too busy. Why is there a nagging thought in my head when I do take time out in my day to pray, that I have things I need to be getting on with? It takes discipline to prioritise prayer.

Craig Groeschel says making small changes over time creates great change.

Why not think about one new discipline in prayer that you can begin?

Commit to it for at least one month.

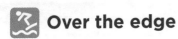 # Over the edge

Here are two absolutely brilliant passages of the Bible:

> *'If my people who are called by my name humble themselves and pray and seek my face and turn from their wicked ways, I will hear from heaven and forgive their sin and heal their land.'* (2 Chronicles 7:14)

> *'If we confess our sins, he is faithful and just and will forgive us our sins and purify us from all unrighteousness.'* (I John 1:9)

When we ask God to forgive us barriers are removed enabling us to enjoy a closer intimacy with God. When we withhold forgiveness we create barriers to God acting on our behalf to our prayers. Its a good idea to start with forgiveness as we see modelled in the Lords prayer.

Effective prayer is also made possible by our mediator, Jesus.

> *'For there is one God and one mediator between God and mankind, the man Christ Jesus'* (1 Timothy 2:5)

Hebrews 10:19 tells us we can have confidence to enter the presence of God.

Faith-filled, bold prayers can change things.

Make the decision to pray about something beyond your capability to change or fix. Write it down and commit to pray for it in faith every day until you see the breakthrough.

Session 2: Unlimited Authority

 Straight from the heart

When selling our house a few years ago and after spending the day cleaning the place from top to bottom, the first couple came in, didn't really look at the place and walked out. I asked God if the next person or couple who came around to look could be the buyers as I could not keep spending a day cleaning to make the house presentable. I asked because I had a seven-year-old and an eight-month-old baby and had just returned back to work on the outskirts of London which was a two and a half hour commute each way. The next couple who came did buy the house.

Another time I had no car and a very small budget and had been asking God to help. I felt challenged to be specific and thankful in my request. After numerous prayer times I felt annoyed that nothing seemed to be happening and complained to God. His response was, 'I'm waiting for you to tell me the colour.' Indignantly I said 'green.' Two days later I purchased my green Citroen Picasso for £350 - incredibly cheap. When I opened the door to look inside, there was an air freshener with words on it stating 'keep the faith.' Humble thanks given.

Julie Botwright

Read the passage:

When Jesus had finished saying all this to the people who were listening, he entered Capernaum. There a centurion's servant, whom his master valued highly, was sick and about to die. The centurion heard of Jesus and sent some elders of the Jews to him, asking him to come and heal his servant. When they came to Jesus, they pleaded earnestly with him, "This man deserves to have you do this, because he loves our nation and has built our synagogue." So Jesus went with them.

He was not far from the house when the centurion sent friends to say to him: "Lord, don't trouble yourself, for I do not deserve to have you come under my roof. That is why I did not even consider myself worthy to come to you. But say the word, and my servant will be healed. For I myself am a man under authority, with soldiers under me. I tell this one, 'Go,' and he goes; and that one, 'Come,' and he comes. I say to my servant, 'Do this,' and he does it."

When Jesus heard this, he was amazed at him, and turning to the crowd following him, he said, "I tell you, I have not found such great faith even in Israel." Then the men who had been sent returned to the house and found the servant well.

Luke 7:1-10

Connect

Who are we praying to? One of the ways God reveals who he is, is by his names.

Write out the names of God (below) and their meanings on separate pieces of paper, one set for each team. The challenge for the teams is to be the first to match names and meanings correctly. For added difficulty you can add the Bible references to be matched up too.

Jehovah Jireh	The Lord provides	Genesis 22:14
Jehovah Rapha	The Lord that heals	Exodus 15:26, Psalm 103:3
Jehovah Nissi	The Lord our banner	Exodus 17:15
Jehovah Shalom	The Lord our peace	Judges 6:24
Jehovah Rohi	The Lord our shepherd	Psalm 23:1
Jehovah Tsiadkeniu	The Lord our righteousness	Jeremiah 23:6
Jehovah Shammah	The Lord is present	Ezekiel 48:35, Hebrews 13:5
Jehovah M Kaddesh	The Lord who sanctifies	Leviticus 20:7-8
Jehovah Adonai	The Lord who is master	Psalm 91:1
Jehovah El Shaddai	The Lord all sufficient	Genesis 49:25

> **Prayer is our weapon of warfare, our weapon to enforce heaven's rule.**
>
> **Prayer can change things in a powerful way and we are those who can pray those prayers. Prayer is part of God's plan and purpose for our lives as His children to partner with Him in bringing his Kingdom rule.**
>
> Judith Annis

 Creating space

My thoughts and notes...

I love this account of the Centurion and how it illustrates what God's authority means for us.

I can remember my son coming home from School one day and telling me, "Mum you always tell me mums know everything, but you don't know everything, only my teacher does!" That was the day I realised his view of my authority would never be the same again. He no longer believed I had all the answers; he had begun the journey along the road to independence.

We are to come to God as children, with complete trust and faith. Praying with authority isn't dependent on how good, qualified or radical we are but rather on who we believe God is and how we believe he sees us. We don't grow in independence from him but rather we are called to grow more dependent on him.

As we grow in intimacy with God, our prayers change from a simple 'I love you' to 'I love you and I want to invest in all that you want to invest in.'

To be able to pray with authority we need to pray in faith. That faith is grounded in the confidence we have in Jesus' authority over every opposing power, sickness and disease. It's the confidence that Jesus' blood has paid the price for the weak, the broken and the unqualified (me), to stand in his presence and be used as vessels for his glory.

We serve a God who has unlimited authority. He has already won the battle.

He fights on our behalf.

You will not have to fight this battle. Take up your positions; stand firm and see the deliverance the Lord will give you, Judah and Jerusalem. Do not be afraid; do not be discouraged. Go out to face them tomorrow, and the Lord will be with you. (2 Chronicles 20:17)

But thanks be to God! He gives us the victory through our Lord Jesus Christ. (1 Corinthians 15:57)

In this world you will have trouble. But take heart! I have overcome the world. (John 16:33)

> *Prayer is enveloped intimacy and engaged involvement, dutiful discipline and deepest delight. It is whispered breath and wildest battle cry. It is access, authority and awe filled adoration. It aches and agonises for Kingdom come. It bellows and beseeches for his will to be done. Prayer is the engine room that drives the propellers of omnipotence.*
>
> Phil Knox

 **Eat it up**

Look up the dictionary definition of 'authority.'

What is authority?

Can you think of some good examples of those who act under authority (such as the Prime Minister, the police or a football referee)? What is the result of their working under authority?

The Centurion understood being under authority. He himself was a servant of Caesar and had soldiers under his command. He exercised Caesar's authority as he commanded his soldiers, and the power given to him when acting under that authority. God gives authority to us. That authority though, does come with responsibility and accountability.

On an American football pitch it might seem the big strong players are the important ones but actually it's the little referee who has the power. He has the authority on the pitch.

God's authority

Read Romans 8:37-39

> *'No, in all these things we are more than conquerors through him who loved us. For I am convinced that neither death nor life, neither angels nor demons, neither the present nor the future, nor any powers, neither height nor depth, nor anything else in all creation, will be able to separate us from the love of God that is in Christ Jesus our Lord.'*

And read Ephesians 1:18-23

> *I pray that the eyes of your heart may be enlightened in order that you may know the hope to which he has called you, the riches of his glorious inheritance in his holy people, 'and his incomparably great power for us who believe. That power is the same as the mighty strength he exerted*

*when he raised Christ from the dead
and seated him at his right hand in the
heavenly realms, far above all rule and
authority, power and dominion, and
every name that is invoked, not only in
the present age but also in the one to
come. And God placed all things under
his feet and appointed him to be head
over everything for the church, which
is his body, the fullness of him who fills
everything in every way.'*

Our authority

God has given us his power, and the faith to
believe that Jesus has qualified us to show
God's glory. God desires that we show his glory
and use his power even more than we do.

We exercise our authority in faith - not faith in
ourselves, but in God.

Read Mark 11:23-24

*Truly I tell you, if anyone says to this
mountain, 'Go, throw yourself into
the sea,' and does not doubt in their
heart but believes that what they say
will happen, it will be done for them.
Therefore I tell you, whatever you ask
for in prayer, believe that you have
received it, and it will be yours.*

When we know the Bible, we can confidently
pray in line with God's will, and therefore with
his authority. When we believe his word and
his character, we pray full of faith that he can
answer.

God Word is full of so many promises for our
lives. There are many times we have not seen
the fulfillment of his promises. We are called
to pray in faith standing on the authority God
has given to us to bring the fulfillment of
those promises. We pray knowing the battle is
already won as God already has all authority.
He fights on our behalf, as Jesus intercedes for
us.

Romans 8:34 says:

*Who then is the one who condemns?
No one. Christ Jesus who died—more
than that, who was raised to life—is*

at the right hand of God and is also interceding for us.

Prayer is our secret weapon. Prayer can break through to places we cannot even begin to impact. Prayer is a missile that can travel faster than the speed of light or thought. It always brings a change.

Our prayers can change the future. We can pray for our children and those prayers are an inheritance for their future, even if they are answered long after we have gone.

Prayer is a weapon Satan has no defence against. He cannot penetrate our prayers to our father.

We have all we need. God has already promised it to us but we have to pray to get hold of it. God does his part but we also have a part to play – prayer!

Ask yourself, how much of my prayer life is focused on the authority God has and the authority he has given me?

Read these verses together about God's power and authority given to you.

How does this change your prayers?

> *But I will come to you very soon, if the Lord is willing, and then I will find out not only how these arrogant people are talking, but what power they have. For the kingdom of God is not a matter of talk but of power.*
> (1 Corinthians 4:19-20)

> *...and in Christ you have been brought to fullness. He is the head over every power and authority.*
> (Colossians 2:10)

> *I pray that out of his glorious riches he may strengthen you with power through his Spirit in your inner being, so that Christ may dwell in your hearts through faith. And I pray that you, being rooted and established in love, may have power, together with all the Lord's holy people, to grasp how wide and long and high and deep is*

the love of Christ, and to know this love that surpasses knowledge—that you may be filled to the measure of all the fullness of God. Now to him who is able to do immeasurably more than all we ask or imagine, according to his power that is at work within us, to him be glory in the church and in Christ Jesus throughout all generations, for ever and ever! Amen.
(Ephesians 3:16-21)

Adam and Eve were given authority over creation until they disobeyed God:

'Then God said, "Let us make mankind in our image, in our likeness, so that they may rule over the fish in the sea and the birds in the sky, over the livestock and all the wild animals, and over all the creatures that move along the ground."'
(Genesis 1:26)

It was always God's plan for us to work in relationship and partnership with him.

 No human endeavour can achieve the things that can only be made a reality through prayer.

Mike Andrea

Give it up

In the second part of Mark 11:23, Jesus says, *but believe that what they say will happen, it will be done for them'* [emphasis ours].

There is something important about saying things out loud, not just thinking them. Faith comes through hearing. That includes hearing yourself say the truth too.

Spend some time declaring who God is and what that means to you.

If you are in a group why not also make some declarations over each other.

 # Empowered life

Courtroom authority

It may help you to imagine the authority that is carried in a courtroom. There is a set order and purpose. The practical authority given to the court is known as jurisdication - the power to decide certain kinds of petitions and questions put to it.

There is a lot of legal and governance language used in the Bible. In Luke 18 (verses 1:8), Jesus tells a parable about a judge to teach about persistence in prayer:

> *'Then Jesus told his disciples a parable to show them that they should always pray and not give up. He said: "In a certain town there was a judge who neither feared God nor cared what people thought. And there was a widow in that town who kept coming to him with the plea, 'Grant me justice against my adversary.'*
>
> *"For some time he refused. But finally he said to himself, 'Even though I don't fear God or care what people think, yet because this widow keeps bothering me, I will see that she gets justice, so that she won't eventually come and attack me!'"*
>
> *And the Lord said, "Listen to what the unjust judge says. And will not God bring about justice for his chosen ones, who cry out to him day and night? Will he keep putting them off? I tell you, he will see that they get justice, and quickly. However, when the Son of Man comes, will he find faith on the earth?'*

Take some time to study some of these Bible verses. What picture do they paint?

Revelation 4: 6	Throne of God
Ephesians 1:20	Jesus seated
Ephesians 2:6	Us seated
Hebrews 12:1	Cloud of witnesses
Philippians 4:3	The book of life
Revelation 12:18	Our accuser
Matthew 5:25	Answer the accuser
1 John 2:1	Jesus our advocate

 **Over the edge**

In what areas of your life would you like to see breakthrough? Is that breakthrough in line with God's promises for his children?

Take some time to look up the verses that give you the promises for that breakthrough and prepare a case for the legal right for that breakthrough.

You could use the picture you built up from the previous section to enter into heaven's courts by faith to get heaven's agreement.

The Bible tells us to be quick to answer your accuser. Spend some time in repentance for any area you may have come into agreement with the enemy. This can be an area of offence, unforgiveness or wrong actions. Repent of any area that you have believed less than God's word in and then enter the courtroom remembering that Jesus is your advocate and present your case.

Pray God's word back to him. Pray it as a declaration.

You might want to write out some of the declarations to repeat daily. Put them up on your mirror or on the fridge.

Session 3: Unlimited Pursuit

 ## Straight from the heart

My husband had a persistent cough – really bad. I am always losing him in supermarkets and I would just stop, listen and follow the cough. Nowadays I have to ring his mobile because after being referred to hospital and diagnosed with bronchiectasis, which is an incurable lung disease that produces loads of phlegm, we realised one day that he had simply stopped coughing. This was after much persistent and heartfelt prayer. In fact, his chest is so good now, one of our local doctors was recently questioning the diagnosis. During this period, in an effort to unblock the catarrh in his left ear he blew his nose so violently he deafened himself. The hospital said the damage was irreparable and his hearing loss was permanent, so they took moulds for a hearing aid that might help a little bit. It was frustrating for both of us because communicating was so difficult and in certain circumstances he would not hear in spite of my shouting! Again, persistent prayer paid off and it was actually in a prayer meeting that his hearing was fully restored. He kept the appointment to have the aid fitted but told them he felt a fraud because he could hear after being prayed for. They said, "we have explained to you that the damage to your Eustachian tube is irreversible but OK we will do another test". After the test they said, "Mr Carvosso, you have your miracle!"

Mandy Carvosso

Read the passage:

Now the tax collectors and sinners were all gathering around to hear Jesus. But the Pharisees and the teachers of the law muttered, "This man welcomes sinners and eats with them." Then Jesus told them this parable: "Suppose one of you has a hundred sheep and loses one of them. Doesn't he leave the ninety-nine in the open country and go after the lost sheep until he finds it? And when he finds it, he joyfully puts it on his shoulders and goes home. Then he calls his friends and neighbours together and says, 'Rejoice with me; I have found my lost sheep.' I tell you that in the same way there will be more rejoicing in heaven over one sinner who repents than over ninety-nine righteous persons who do not need to repent.

Luke 15:1-7

 ## Connect

Play 'The Potato Icebreaker'

Give each person a medium sized potato and a straw (an eco-friendly one). Tell the group:

A key to following through is the faith to believe that it's possible.

Ask 'how many of you believe you can drive your straw through your potato with a single blow?'

The secret is 'follow through'.

Hold the straw in a closed fist with your thumb over the top. Put your arm at the side.

In your other hand, cup the potato so hand forms a 'C' around it. Don't hold it in the palm of your hand for safety! Hold your arm in front at a good angle for the straw to take aim!

Bending elbow, draw hand with straw back, and then on the count of three, lunge forward, at the same time, yell "follow through". Don't aim at the surface of the potato but aim past (through the other side of the potato).

(Do a couple of 'practice' lunges without the potato to build confidence.) Teaching points:

Some of the group will be successful. Others will need another straw and another try.

Keep pursuing until we see the breakthrough. Believe for it in faith without hesitation.

Through prayer we connect with God, expressing our deepest longings, pain and desires. It's the safest of places. We scope out our dreams and enjoy the perspective of the divine 'sounding board'. We share our delights and find comfort in our sufferings. Through prayer we find answers when needed and peace when there's no answer that can calm our troubled souls. Prayer is the partner of action. Their partnership together enables us to walk God's way and make this world a better place.

Roger Ellis

 # Creating space

God is in relentless pursuit of us. We may not be seeking him but he has not and will not stop pursuing us.

'Your beauty and love chase after me every day of my life.'
(Psalm 23:6 -The Message)

'We love because he first loved us.'
(1 John 4:19)

I love the lyrics of the song 'Reckless Love' by Steffany Gretzinger, Bethel Music. It speaks of this never-ending pursuit God has for us.

You were created with a God-given desire for connection with him. Your spirit is hungry for prayer. Prayer is the breath of God in your life.

Read Luke 11:9-13

> *"So I say to you: Ask and it will be given to you; seek and you will find; knock and the door will be opened to you. For everyone who asks receives; the one who seeks finds; and to the one who knocks, the door will be opened.*

> *"Which of you fathers, if your son asks for[a] a fish, will give him a snake instead? Or if he asks for an egg, will give him a scorpion? If you then, though you are evil, know how to give good gifts to your children, how much more will your Father in heaven give the Holy Spirit to those who ask him!"*

As we pray we chase God's presence, chasing after the fresh thing God is doing. Prayer enables us to find out what God is up to and pursue it - in stillness but also in movement. As we have already looked at, prayer requires faith.

French philosopher and mathematician, Blaise Pascal, observed that most of our human problems come because we don't know how to sit still in our room for an hour.

Jesus asked the disciples in Gethsemane to keep watch. He meant 'Be still in prayer with me. Do not fall asleep!'

When we face troubles and trials it can be those things that actually cause us to press harder into God. When we need him we chase him. We would do better to chase him always so when we need him we know we already have him.

 ## Eat it up

Are our lives an endless pursuit of God? If they were what would that look like?

Look at these Bible verses together to see just some of the ways the Bible says to pursue God.

How did Jesus find out what God's will for him was?

- *'One of those days Jesus went out to a mountainside to pray, and spent the night praying to God. Before appointing the twelve he spent the night in prayer to his father. He often withdrew to lonely places and prayed.'* (Luke 6:12)

- *'But Jesus often withdrew to lonely places and prayed.'* (Luke 5:16)

How do we sustain the pursuit of God?

- *Then Jesus told his disciples a parable to show them that they should always pray and not give up.* (Luke 18:1)

- *I tell you, even though he will not get up and give you the bread because of friendship, yet because of your shameless audacity he will surely get up and give you as much as you need. 9 "So I say to you: Ask and it will be given to you; seek and you will find; knock and the door will be opened to you.* (Luke 11: 8-9)

- *'I looked for someone among them who would build up the wall and stand before me in the gap on behalf of the land so I would not have to destroy it, but I found no one.'* (Ezekiel 22:30)

God is looking for those who will have the faith to stand in the gap between the seen and not yet seen and believe and pray in faith for what is not yet seen.

> *'If my people, who are called by my name, will humble themselves and pray and seek my face and turn from their wicked ways, then I will hear from heaven, and I will forgive their sin and will heal their land.'* (2 Chronicles 7:14)

> ❝ *Prayer gives God a clear road for action. I cannot - will not - must not - ever give up being persistent especially in the face of impossibility.* ❞
>
> Maddy Carvosso

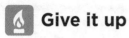 # Give it up

As we dwell on the beauty and greatness of God there is a transformation that happens in our heart. Our prayers flow out of a relationship with him but thankfulness opens the gates. (Psalm 100:4)

We can see in the Psalms many prayers that start with despair and woe but as the psalmist writes we see as they begin to remember the good things God has done and bring thanks for these, their despair turns to hope.

> *Take delight in the Lord, and he will give you the desires of your heart.*
> (Psalm 37:4)

If there are difficulties you are facing or pain you are feeling, you can be honest before God just as we see in Psalms. Take some time to write your own psalm.

Think about different aspects of you and of God. Use your senses: sights, sounds, and fragrances. Think about relationships, culture, society or your day. Allow yourself to be poetic. Don't be afraid to make mistakes as this will hinder your creativity. Put some worship or instrumental music on whilst you do this.

If you feel brave enough, read your psalms aloud and then pray for each other.

 # Empowered life

Read Psalm 91

There are so many promises here that you can dwell on and remind God of as you seek him in prayer. If you feel you don't know how to pray, then use this Psalm. Say it out loud! When we hear, we believe. Our brains react to hearing the word.

Isaiah 62, "Remind the Lord day and night."

We already have God's spirit in us so why should we remind the Lord day and night? It is more about reminding ourselves. Of course, God doesn't need reminding but we do. We remind him with thankfulness to stir our Spirit.

Remind God of his promises. Seek out what his word says and set your heart on pursuing those promises.

Our prayer is not to persuade God to do what we want him to do but it's to remind ourselves of his promises and to thank him for them. Prayer helps us to see what has already been given to us in the spiritual realm come into being in the natural realm.

This kind of prayer builds our faith and helps build perseverance.

Over the edge

After Jesus had returned to heaven, the disciples waited in an upper room. Is this like your church prayer meeting? Are you a bunch of people from all walks of life gathered together in one place? They weren't bold, they didn't know what was going to happen, they were maybe a little disheartened but they were obedient and they waited.

The most uninspired prayer gathering turned into the most powerful, inspiring, awe-filled, life changing, community changing, world changing event.

The Holy Spirit fell. Fire came, they began to speak in tongues, the community was awakened, boldness was given and the gospel, the good news about Jesus went forth.

Will you wait, with faith, for God to come in power as he has promised? Will you commit to waiting expectantly on him for that same power we know he has already invested in us but have not yet seen in fullness? Are you willing for your life to be changed? Why not commit to the pursuit of God for more of him?

Take some time to ask God what more of him in your life would be like.

Session 4: Unlimited Hope

> **Prayer straightens my wobbly thoughts, reorientates my being to hope, soothes my heart to let go and sleep.**
>
> Maggie Ellis

Straight from the heart

After teaching for 20 years I decided to make a change last year. I was stressed and unhappy in my job all the time. I didn't have a clue what else I could do. I began praying and asking for God's guidance and help. After a few months I started to think I would enjoy an admin job but I had no idea where to look for one. I stuck a post-it note on my bedroom wall saying, 'I'm praying for an admin job' and then trawled through job sites not getting very inspired. Every day I would ask God to show me what to do and I read and prayed through verses about God's plans for me.

Well, God had a plan for me and I ended up getting the administrator's position in our church. Six months on, I am the happiest I've ever been and know to trust God with every decision in my life. Prayer changes things and opens up opportunities.

Sharon Marriott

Read the passage:

"Do not let your hearts be troubled. You believe in God; believe also in me. My Father's house has many rooms; if that were not so, would I have told you that I am going there to prepare a place for you? And if I go and prepare a place for you, I will come back and take you to be with me that you also may be where I am. You know the way to the place where I am going."

Jesus the Way to the Father

Thomas said to him, "Lord, we don't know where you are going, so how can we know the way?"

Jesus answered, "I am the way and the truth and the life. No one comes to the Father except through me. 7 If you really know me, you will know my Father as well. From now on, you do know him and have seen him."

Philip said, "Lord, show us the Father and that will be enough for us."

Jesus answered: "Don't you know me, Philip, even after I have been among you such a long time? Anyone who has seen me has seen the Father. How can you say, 'Show us the Father'? Don't you believe that I am in the Father, and that the Father is in me? The words I say to you I do not speak on my own authority.

Rather, it is the Father, living in me, who is doing his work. Believe me when I say that I am in the Father and the Father is in me; or at least believe on the evidence of the works themselves. Very truly I tell you, whoever believes in me will do the works I have been doing, and they will do even greater things than these, because I am going to the Father. And I will do whatever you ask in my name, so that the Father may be glorified in the Son. You may ask me for anything in my name, and I will do it.

John 14:1-14

 # Connect

What are your God-given hopes and dreams?

You will need pens and paper for everyone.

Allow time for people to write down their hopes and dreams for the future (warning - these will be shared later).

Everyone then folds up his or her piece of paper and places it in a hat or bowl.

Pass the hat around and take it in turns to pick out a piece of paper and guess who wrote it.

Now take some time either as a group or in pairs to pray over the hopes and dreams that have been expressed.

If you want a greater challenge the group can ask God what he wants to say to each person with regard to their hopes and dreams. Take some time to share what people hear for each other. (Remember this is a safe space to have a go and make mistakes as we practise listening to God together).

If there are members of the group who feel they find it hard to hear from God then ask them to share their greatest encouragement for the person.

 # Creating space

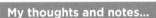
My thoughts and notes...

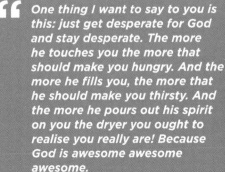

> *One thing I want to say to you is this: just get desperate for God and stay desperate. The more he touches you the more that should make you hungry. And the more he fills you, the more that he should make you thirsty. And the more he pours out his spirit on you the dryer you ought to realise you really are! Because God is awesome awesome awesome.*
>
> Bonnie Chavda

I think we have learned a few things about prayer over our years of following Jesus and leading church and yes, we could tell you many stories of answered prayer, but we definitely don't have it all together. Our lives are often as messy as anyone else's. We have arguments; we didn't stop and pray when we would have been better off doing so! Like everyone else, we sometimes messed up with our kids sometimes. Often, we just haven't had the faith or have been like yoyos in belief and then in unbelief. One thing is for sure - we still have a lot to learn.

I feel encouraged when I look at the disciples and see that even though they had spent time with Jesus and he had taught them so much they were still weak and had so much to learn. As Jesus spent the last night with them, they were afraid of being left alone. One of them said, 'Lord show us the father and that will be enough for us' (John 14:8). He wanted to see with physical sight not just by faith.

This is how Jesus answered him:

> *"Don't you know me, Philip, even after I have been among you such a long time? Anyone who has seen me has seen the Father. How can you say, 'Show us the Father'? Don't you believe that I am in the Father, and that the Father is in me? The words I say to you I do not speak on my own authority. Rather, it is the Father, living in me, who is doing his work. Believe me when I say that I am in the Father and the Father is in me; or at least believe on the evidence of the works themselves."* (John 14:9-11)

Jesus was telling them he did nothing in his own strength but in his Father's. In Jesus' name we can have access to the same strength (and even greater - John 14:12) through the Holy Spirit, and we have Jesus interceding on our behalf too.

I get so excited when I read the book of Acts and see what God did through Jesus' disciples and the early church. I am excited because it gives me hope for the church today. It gives me hope that I can hold onto God's promise that even more good things are to come. I am excited to see the impossible happening today, in our lives, in our churches, in our communities. God is a God of the impossible and signs, wonders and miracles are to follow those who follow him. That's us!

It's so freeing to know I am not responsible for the breakthrough, signs, wonders and miracles myself. I am not responsible for making them happen. My only responsibility is to know God's ability and respond to that. I get the privilege of opening the door for God to step in.

My focus needs to stay on him and my devotion to him. As I spend time in his presence I can be transformed. I can release the kingdom around me because I know who God is and because I know I am loved.

Even when we are still waiting for the breakthrough to come, we wait in faith in who he is. Our challenge is to resist changing our perception of who God is to fit with our experience and instead changing who we are to position ourselves more in his presence; to be more overwhelmed with him than ourselves, to be full of faith in who he is and his promises for each one of us.

> **I have been so grateful to have the privilege of prayer in my life; it has saved me from many a poor decision or cross word.**
>
> **It has given me the ability to have peace and I would say no matter where or what you find yourself in, keep praying.**
>
> Jess Soames

 # Eat it up

Are there times you have not seen answers to prayer?

Be honest about how you have handled this.

Has it led you to change your belief about who God is or has it made you more desperate to press into God for breakthrough?

How can we support one another in the prayers that we have not yet seen answers to? The following verses may help you think about this:

> *But encourage one another daily, as long as it is called "Today," so that none of you may be hardened by sin's deceitfulness.* (Hebrews 3:13)

> *Again, truly I tell you that if two of you on earth agree about anything they ask for, it will be done for them by my Father in heaven. For where two or three gather in my name, there am I with them.* (Matthew 18:19-20)

 ## Give it up

We have to work to not let disappointment, or fear of disappointment, get in the way of trusting God. Stay unoffended, as offence is a trick of the enemy to make us lose hope.

 Love forgets wrongs so that there is hope for the future...

When those who have been placed in my life to lead me and train me betray me and turn against me, as Saul turned against David, I will follow the example of David and refuse to let hope die in my heart.

John Bevere

Offence, unforgiveness and disappointment all rob us of hope. The Bible says that Satan roams the earth looking for believers to devour (1 Peter 5:8). If he can rob us of hope then our future looks bleak.

 The person with the most hope has the most influence.

Bill Johnson

Read these verses together:

Consider it pure joy, my brothers and sisters, whenever you face trials of many kinds, 3 because you know that the testing of your faith produces perseverance.4 Let perseverance finish its' work so that you may be mature and complete, not lacking anything.
(James 1:2-4)

I pray also that the eyes of your heart may be enlightened in order that you may know the hope to which he has called you, the riches of his glorious inheritance in the saints, and his incomparably great power for us who believe. That power is like the working of his mighty strength, which he exerted in Christ when he raised him from the dead and seated him at his right hand in the heavenly realms, far above all rule and authority, power and dominion, and every title that can be given, not only in the present age but also in the one to come. And God placed all things under his feet and appointed him to be head over everything for the church; which is his body, the fullness of him who fills everything in every way.
(Ephesians 1:18-23)

May the God of hope fill you with all joy and peace as you trust in him, so that you may overflow with hope by the power of the Holy Spirit. (Romans 15:13)

If we lose our joy and begin to feel hopelessness creeping in, in any area of life, in my experience, it's always best to start with a prayer to ask for forgiveness and to search our hearts to see if there is anyone we need to forgive.

Take some time to either work through these questions in pairs or on your own.

Is there an area of your life where you are feeling hopeless?

Pray through a forgiveness prayer such as:

Father God because of your forgiveness of me I choose to forgive...

I choose to forgive them for their words or actions.

I choose to forgive them for the door they have opened to... (maybe pain, suffering, lies, self-doubt).

Ask God if there is a lie you are believing as a result of their words or actions.

Sit quietly and take time to listen for an answer.

Ask him what his truth is about the situation.

Pray a blessing over the person.

Empowered life

Unfortunately, God never said we wouldn't have troubles.

We live in a complaining culture, everyone complains and moans about lots of things but I want to encourage you that the place to take your complaint is to God.

The complaint you have may be about your wife, your husband, your children, your boss at work, someone in your family, your neighbour, your church leader, that person in your class, somebody else in church who is winding you up, or the person who is pushing all the wrong buttons. The best person to take your complaint to is God, in prayer. It is most likely when we are afflicted, troubled and downtrodden, that complaints will come to the surface. In the book of James we are encouraged to find faith and hope in difficulties through prayer.

Prayer and worship help us find grace in those difficult times. It is important to watch what comes out of our mouth in hard times.

> *The tongue has the power of life and death, and those who love it will eat its fruit.* (Proverbs 18:21)

> *For his anger lasts only a moment, but his favour lasts a lifetime. Weeping may last through the night, but joy comes in the morning.* (Psalm 30:5)

In prosperity, when things are going well, sing the psalms, worship God, thank him for all he is doing. If today is a good day, rejoice and be glad in it, for tomorrow it may not be a good day. In the Christian life, it isn't about how many good days we can get out of the week. It is about how we can pray and worship throughout our week whatever the days look like. The challenging thing is for us to worship at all times whether things are good or bad. It is not just about when it is a nice sunny day, it is worshipping when in our heart there is cheerfulness or sadness. We should always be content in God.

As we keep our focus on our King we will see the kingdom come, giving Jesus the glory, honour, love and respect as we journey.

Sometimes all we can do is pray for strength to endure the trial staying faithful to Jesus.

Nehemiah 8:10 says the 'joy of the Lord is [our] strength'. One of the fruits of the spirit is joy. We can ask for it, petition God for it and thank God for it in faith.

Why not practice a complaint fast this week (or even for a day). Every time you may want to voice or even think a complaint make a declaration of God's goodness and thankfulness to him instead and see how your joy increases! Keep a note of it. Look back at the end of the day and be encouraged.

Here are some declarations based on Bible verses to get you started:

- 'I set the course of my life with my words.' (James 3:2-5)

- 'I have a sound mind and today I will think great thoughts with understanding and wisdom.' (2 Timothy 1:7)

- 'Today I will see God move through me to touch other people's lives.' (Mark 16:17-18)

- 'I am a child of God. It's who he says I am that matters.' (Romans 8:16)

- 'I can do this. I am strong enough and brave enough.' (Philippians 4:13)

Over the edge

Prayer breaks us out of our normal expectations and limitations. We see the fruits of the spirit grow in our lives - love, joy, peace, patience, gentleness, faithfulness, kindness, goodness and self control.

Life is not just about the external things making us happy; it is also necessary that we protect our heart so that our heart is cheerful.

How is your heart today?

Is your heart still? Is your heart happy? Is your heart troubled?

Is your heart cheerful in God?

Are you cheering yourself on in the Lord?

Take some time in prayer to seek God for your heart. When all is well with our soul we are more effective in God's kingdom.

Be still.

You may find this technique will help you:

Select a word or scripture. (I like to say the name Jesus).

Find a quiet place where you can get comfortable.

Close your eyes and just concentrate on breathing slowly.

Begin to be aware of your breathing. Breathe in through your nose and out through your mouth, with slow, deep breaths.

Be aware of any tension in your body and relax those areas as you breathe out.

Begin to focus on the word or scripture.

Continue and if your mind begins to wander to shopping lists and to-do lists that's OK but just bring your thinking back to focus on the word or scripture.

Do this for five to 20 minutes.

Be expectant for God to say something to you.

It may be as simple as experiencing peace or it may be inspiration or wisdom on a subject you have been seeking answers to or it may be a random inspiration to contact someone. Try not to expect God to only speak to you one way. He is a creative God!

Straight from the heart

I was saved at the Downs Bible Week in Sussex and would go and help out each year in the children's tent and shop. One year I was sitting in a friend's caravan when she showed me an article about a sweet family of four with another four adopted children. I was really interested being adopted myself. I was drawn to them and said out loud, 'I would really like to get to know them.' I prayed that I would meet this family. Eighteen years later, happily married with my own family in a small farmhouse in very rural Norfolk we had only one neighbour just up the hill. They were new and we went to introduce ourselves on our way home from school. When I realised they were the family I had wanted to get to know all that time ago, my neighbour became my best friend, prayer partner, confidante, comforter, mum, a friend and person I knew I could always trust and rely on. My friend, her husband and all the children (now grown) have been an inspiration to me and my family. God knew how important this family would be to me all those years ago. This relationship is now 13 years old and ongoing. My prayer was answered in a more wonderful way than I had imagined. God is a good father and is full of surprises.

Frances Cheer

Read the passage:

Then Elijah said to all the people, "Come here to me." They came to him, and he repaired the altar of the Lord, which had been torn down. Elijah took twelve stones, one for each of the tribes descended from Jacob, to whom the word of the Lord had come, saying, "Your name shall be Israel." With the stones he built an altar in the name of the Lord, and he dug a trench around it large enough to hold two seahs[a] of seed. He arranged the wood, cut the bull into pieces and laid it on the wood. Then he said to them, "Fill four large jars with water and pour it on the offering and on the wood."

"Do it again," he said, and they did it again.

"Do it a third time," he ordered, and they did it the third time. The water ran down around the altar and even filled the trench.

At the time of sacrifice, the prophet Elijah stepped forward and prayed: "Lord, the God of Abraham, Isaac and Israel, let it be known today that you are God in Israel and that I am your servant and have done all these things at your command.Answer me, Lord, answer me, so these people will know that you, Lord, are God, and that you are turning their hearts back again."

Then the fire of the Lord fell and burned up the sacrifice, the wood, the stones and the soil, and also licked up the water in the trench.

When all the people saw this, they fell prostrate and cried, "The Lord—he is God! The Lord—he is God!"

Then Elijah commanded them, "Seize the prophets of Baal. Don't let anyone get away!" They seized them, and Elijah had them brought down to the Kishon Valley and slaughtered there.

And Elijah said to Ahab, "Go, eat and drink, for there is the sound of a heavy rain." So Ahab went off to eat and drink, but Elijah climbed to the top of Carmel, bent down to the ground and put his face between his knees.

"Go and look toward the sea," he told his servant. And he went up and looked. "There is nothing there," he said.

Seven times Elijah said, "Go back."

The seventh time the servant reported, "A cloud as small as a man's hand is rising from the sea."

So Elijah said, "Go and tell Ahab, 'Hitch up your chariot and go down before the rain stops you.'"

Meanwhile, the sky grew black with clouds, the wind rose, a heavy rain started falling and Ahab rode off to Jezreel. The power of the Lord came on Elijah and, tucking his cloak into his belt, he ran ahead of Ahab all the way to Jezreel.

1 Kings 18:30-46

 # Connect

Play 'Nine Dot Challenge'.

Give everyone a pen and paper and ask them to draw nine dots as seen below (or you could prepare a few for each person):

● ● ●

● ● ●

● ● ●

With a pen or pencil, try to connect all nine dots with only four continuous straight lines or fewer, without lifting the pen and without tracing over the line more than once.

Solution:

This puzzle demonstrates out of the box thinking. For the solution people have to travel with the pen outside of the box they see in front of them.

Often, we limit how we see God and limit our expectation to what we have already seen or experienced.

Creating space

 Prayer is a door for spiritual breakthrough to enter.

Prayer is original research in uncharted territory.

Effective prayer is about a relationship with God that moves beyond monologue to on-going dialogue.

Wayne Drain

We have a Father in heaven who has no limits. He is the God of the impossible, the God of the supernatural. Elijah's life showed what can happen when someone gives themselves to prayer. In these verses we see Elijah pray in public and then in private. The battle was won in prayer. Prayer was the spark that changed a nation.

Elijah was sensitive to the voice of God. He hid when God had told him to remain hidden and he stepped up and presented himself when God said to step out.

Elijah's prayer life with God and his faith and obedience to all God told him to do changed a nation. Through Elijah's obedience God broke into the mess; the disobedience of a nation who had turned away from him.

How we need an Elijah today! Who will be willing to be hidden with God, to pray, to cultivate such sensitivity to his voice, his presence, his power, so that they can stand against culture, popularity, religion and reveal God to a nation?

I have found over the years of following Jesus that as I have spent time in his presence there are many things that once limited my life that are no longer hindrances. God brought about changes in me that led to greater freedom. I also discovered the more I am willing to give away, the more God has for me. It's like a river. If I let it flow – God's presence flowing in me and then out to those around me – the river gets stronger but if I create a dam in the river it begins to stagnate. Often, when the river has begun to stagnate, maybe in a particular area in my life, it's been the prayer of others that's helped dismantle those dams.

I have also discovered that if I surround myself with people who are doing greater things, I am inspired to open the gates wider, to allow more of God into my life. I know there is more, but I also know I always need to pray for more boldness to step out into all God has for me.

There are endless opportunities to grow in faith, to serve more, to give more, to learn more. God wants to bless us not for the sake of blessing but so that we can be a blessing to others. We are called to make a difference, to bring Jesus to our neighbours, our community, our nation, and the world. We need to wait on God to equip us, just as the disciples needed to wait for the Holy Spirit we need to wait to be filled, but it's not a passive waiting. Prayer is never passive.

Remember God is the God of the impossible.

Maybe no one else in your family knows Jesus. He can use you to reveal himself to them. He can use you to speak out his gospel.

Perhaps you have a passion for those in your community who are sick or marginalised. You can be the hands and feet of Jesus. You are already commissioned to heal the sick, raise the dead, cleanse those who have leprosy or drive out demons. Jesus said, *'Freely you have received; freely give.'* (Matthew 10:8)

Remember if it's not a dream that needs God then it's too small a dream. Dream big! Pray big! God rewards faith. It is faith in him, not in ourselves. It is God who qualifies us for what he has called us to.

Eat it up

As a group (or in pairs) ask these questions of each other:

- What are the areas in your family, work place or community you need to see God break into?

- How can you partner with God to be that change?

- Where are the places you are already having an impact and how could that impact be increased?

- There are so many needs as you look around you. What moves you?

You can be sure God is moved more.

Someone once said the things that frustrate you are probably the things God is putting on your heart to change.

Once we have identified what we are passionate to see changed, we can ask God, 'What's stopping me be the change?' You may already know the answer to this without having to ask!

Fear is a common factor that holds us back. Fear of people, fear of failure or fear of not being good enough. Even Paul the apostle had to pray for boldness.

Ungodly habits and behaviour, offense and unforgiveness can also cause blockages.

There may be people in the group who are stuck in an area or find that as much as they want the breakthrough there are certain habits and patterns they cannot break. Don't be afraid to suggest accessing a prayer ministry (maybe you have this in your church) or counselling to help them get unstuck or to work through healing alongside your group praying. God, through the power and counsel of the Holy Spirit, wants to help to remove those barriers as you ask him.

It's good to look at why we want to see these changes, as that will keep us on the right course to see the change happen. The why fuels the passion behind the what!

Ask each other 'why'?

You could keep asking 'why' when they give an answer to really get to the heart of the reason 'why'?

> *When I pray to God I feel that I connect to his heartbeat – when I pray with people I connect with theirs.*
>
> John Hawksworth

 Give it up

For this prayer exercise you will need a map – either of the local area or of the UK. Alternatively, you could mark out the shape of the UK on the floor with string or tape. The bigger the better.

Look at the map and try to find a place or area where you know families and friends live. See where you already have an influence, perhaps through work, travel, or church. Also work out where you see the needs in your community.

Mark those areas with post-it note prayers or, if the map is big enough, move around it standing on the different areas, praying for them as you stand on them.

Pray big, bold prayers!

Empowered life

Again, truly I tell you that if two of you on earth agree about anything they ask for, it will be done for them by my Father in heaven. (Matthew 18:19)

Come together and harmonise in prayer. Prayer is nothing to do with programs or agendas.

Every prayer led by the Holy Spirit will touch the heart of God. Every prayer prayed in line with the word of God will bring change as the Holy Spirit intercedes on our behalf, as it says in Romans 8:26: "In the same way, the Spirit helps us in our weakness. We do not know what we ought to pray for, but the Spirit himself intercedes for us through wordless groans.'

He is sending us out together – one body, one army.

I will stand at my watch

and station myself on the ramparts;

I will look to see what he will say to me,

and what answer I am to give to this complaint. (Habakkuk 2:1)

Prayer is an important foundation in our life and prayer propels our lives to places (both physically and spiritually) we could never have imagined.

Put aside some time this week to sit with a pen and notepad. You can choose your own headers but write some categories (such as the ones below) to complete over the week as you pray and listen to God. This can help your prayer life become a journey and remind you to pray.

- Things I am thankful for (What has God done for you already?)

- Blessings (In what ways has God blessed you this week?)

- Bible verses and impressions (What do you feel God is saying to you, what verses is he highlighting to you?)

- How am I feeling and what's happening this week? (What events are happening? What emotions are you going through?)

- Prayers and petitions (What's God put on your heart to pray for this week and what are the things and people you have already committed to pray for?)

- What's God talking to me about?

- Who have I shared my faith with? (Prayed for, given the gospel to, helped etc.?)

- Answers (What answers have I seen?)

> **" For me, prayer is...**
>
> *"Knowing that I can be completely unmasked and vulnerable yet still loved beyond measure."*
>
> Jenell Chetty

 ## Over the edge

Make a decision to be braver and bolder this week than you were last week.

Take some time to ask for God's guidance and leading.

Dr Billy Graham concluded his book 'The Holy Spirit' with this illustration:

'Over 100 years ago, two young men were talking in Ireland. One said to the other, "The world has yet to see what God will do with a man fully consecrated to him." The other man meditated on that thought for weeks. It so gripped him that one day he exclaimed, "By the Holy Spirit in me, I'll be that man!". Historians now say that he touched two continents for Christ. His name was Dwight L. Moody.'

Each day ask the Holy Spirit to come and fill you afresh and be your guide as you pray.

> *Saul said, "Let us go down and pursue the Philistines by night and plunder them till dawn, and let us not leave one of them alive."*
>
> *"Do whatever seems best to you," they replied.*
>
> *But the priest said, "Let us inquire of God here."*
> (1 Samuel 14:36)
>
> *So David enquired of the Lord...*
> (2 Samuel 5:19)

Perhaps you might want to find a prayer partner to meet up with regularly to challenge each other to act on what you feel God is telling you as you spend time in prayer.

Remember, just as children fall over when they begin to walk it's OK to get things wrong as we practise. Church is a safe place to practise being obedient to God's voice before we take our gifts and callings out to the world.

Remember God is a God of love. He is our greatest encourager. He also wants others to know he loves them and has good things for their lives so if what you feel God is calling you to do is encouraging and life bringing then God's with you.

Straight from the heart

In November 2009, our 18-month-old daughter was diagnosed with cancer. For the next nine months she needed chemotherapy every three weeks for three days. We did not know what the future held for her. Even though, as a church leader, I had often prayed prayers of healing and warfare on behalf of others, I found that in this season I had run out of energy and words to pray like I normally would. I knew others would be praying those kinds of prayers on our behalf and instead I had to find new ways to pray. So, I discovered 'breathing prayers' which were simple but profound. A breathing prayer is a few words that are said in your heart as you breathe in and a few words that are said in your heart as you breathe out. So for many hours, I would sit in a hospital chair with my poorly toddler on my lap, unable to move far as she was attached to a chemotherapy pump that was going directly into her chest via a Hickman line and I would breathe in and say in my heart 'Abba Father' and breathe out and say 'we belong to you.' That particular breathing prayer was an anchor to my soul and enabled me to stay connected to my father through all the questions and uncertainties. I read somewhere at the time that sometimes faith gets redefined as 'walking through the middle of pain and not turning your face away from the Father'. For me, at that time, breathing prayers were a way I could do that.

Ness Wilson

Read the passage:

Bezalel and Oholiab

Then the Lord said to Moses, "See, I have chosen Bezalel son of Uri, the son of Hur, of the tribe of Judah, and I have filled him with the Spirit of God, with wisdom, with understanding, with knowledge and with all kinds of skills— to make artistic designs for work in gold, silver and bronze, to cut and set stones, to work in wood, and to engage in all kinds of crafts. Moreover, I have appointed Oholiab son of Ahisamak, of the tribe of Dan, to help him. Also I have given ability to all the skilled workers to make everything I have commanded you."

Exodus 31:1-6

Connect

M&M Thank-yous

Have a bag of M&M's (or any coloured sweets). Each person takes a sweet. They then let the group know what they are thankful to God for the topic that relates to their colour (see below).

If you want to make it more creative and you have a brave group you could add an action to each one too (offered below in parentheses).

- Red colour: thank God for the favourite things you have done this week. It may be a hobby you've had time for. (Explain it without using the word)

- Green colour: thank God for any provision you've had this week. It could be as simple as the food you've been able to eat. (Mime it)

- Yellow colour: thank God for what he's been speaking to you about this week (Say it)

- Orange colour: thank God for the places you have been to this week. (Draw it)

- Brown colour: thank God for people you have had the opportunity to interact with this week. (Sing it)

- Blue colour: wild cards - they can thank God for anything they choose! (choose an action)

> **Prayer is communication with God and the Bible talks about "praying in the Spirit on all occasions with all kinds of prayers and requests" (Ephesians 6:18).**
>
> **The Holy Spirit longs to open up all sorts of lines of communication with us and for us, let's explore with him the abundance of our relationship with God.**
>
> Pete Carter

 # Creating space

My thoughts and notes...

You could pray the same prayer every day of your life and I am sure God would still love that prayer if it was said in faith. He would love it because he loves you.

We began this study with the Lord's Prayer and it is a great model to use. Jesus gave it to us to pray but there are endless ways you can use it to pray and endless ways to pray it.

God is the creator of the universe, and he made you. We are all so different. We each have different fingerprints; we are all unique.

I believe this creativity and uniqueness gets expressed as we pray. There is no 'one size fits all.' So many resources exist on how to pray, when to pray, what to pray, why to pray and where to pray.

In this final study we take a moment to reflect on how you are so fearfully and wonderfully made. There is no one like you. God will equip you with all you need to pray for each seasonyou find yourself in.

As seasons change in our life, so will the way we pray. There are times when we pray and it feels so easy to connect with God and then suddenly something happens and it doesn't feel easy anymore and vice versa.

Just as the Israelites were provided with manna and led by a cloud and a fire, we can have seasons where provision is easy, answers to prayer are happening daily and then…. and then they entered the Promised Land and provision stopped. They had to work for their food. But of course, it was the Promised Land. It was worth it to take hold of all that was promised.

Don't jump to the conclusion you are doing something wrong if your prayer life feels like there needs to be breakthrough, if what seemed easy before just doesn't feel the same. It's perseverance that builds character, but we must be willing to change how we persevere.

There are seasons God will lead us and the way he communicates with us may change with the season:

> *Forget the former things;*
> *do not dwell on the past.*
>
> *See, I am doing a new thing!*
> *Now it springs up; do you not*
> *perceive it?*
> *I am making a way in the wilderness*
> *and streams in the wasteland.*
> (Isaiah 43: 18-19)

Be ready for the new thing God is doing; be ready for a change of pace of conversation and rhythm.

 # Eat it up

 The Christian shoemaker does his duty not by putting little crosses on the shoes, but by making good shoes, because God is interested in good craftsmanship.

Martin Luther

God is creator and we are made in his image. As co-creators, we can build foundations, birth new ideas and dreams. Words become songs and fill our whole being. Those things only imagined begin to take shape, innovation and inspiration rise up. Words carry across oceans, mountains and into the heavens. Movement begins in response to our desires, as they collide with his. Hope is restored; freedom comes. As our words move his heart, the sick are healed, bodies restored, new neurological pathways are created. Endless possibilities, endless opportunities, as we are touched by our creator God.

You are a new creation. No longer restrained by the laws of this world - an alien in the land.

Just as an acorn that falls to the ground grows to a huge oak tree, so as you submit your life in prayer to God your roots go deep and your faith and life expand. You are new every morning.

Encourage the group that they are God's good craftsmanship and uniquely loved. As we make the sacrifice to spend time with God it ceases to be a sacrifice and becomes a longing. There is no wrong or right way to pray but God looks to the heart. As our thinking lines up with God's word, our heart lines up with God's heart. Let's resolve:

- to be expectant of new ideas, dreams and visions to be given to them both for themselves and others. As we have the faith to act on them the partnership continues to grow.

- to be free to experiment with new and creative ways to pray both alone and with others.

There are many examples of ways to pray in the Bible.

Take a look at these verses.

- 1 Samuel 1:12-13 - Hannah prayed in silence

- Mathew 6:6 - Jesus talks about praying alone

- 1 Thessalonians 5:17 - Pray without ceasing

- Ephesians 6:18 - Praying in the Spirit
- Psalm 139: 1-2 Prayerful thoughts
- Jeremiah 29:12 - Call on God
- Matthew 26:41 - Watch and pray
- Luke 6:12 - Pray through the night
- Romans 8:26 - Pray with wordless groans
- 1 Timothy 2:8 - Pray with hands lifted
- Luke 2:37 - Pray and fast

Share with each other any experience you may have of praying in different ways. Maybe you can find some other ways in scripture.

> **" *I love to pray in the Spirit as I don't always find it easy to express words to describe what is in my head and heart but I find it releasing to express what is in the depths of my being. I love to sing, groan, consider, contemplate and utter sounds to God who knows, understands, loves and acts.* "**
>
> Linda Ward

Give it up

Take some time as a group to pray together.

Is there a theme that has come up as you have completed this study?

Be brave in the way you pray today.

Try a different position physically.

Take some time to allow God to speak as you pray together.

Encourage the group to pray in creative ways together. You may want to use some of the ideas at the back of this guide.

Give each person a pen and paper to record what God is saying (or assign a scribe or press record on your phone if you are speaking out what you feel he is saying).

Empowered life

For we are God's handiwork, created in Christ Jesus to do good works, which God prepared in advance for us to do.
(Ephesians 2:10)

Not only so, but we also glory in our sufferings, because we know that suffering produces perseverance; perseverance, character; and character, hope.
(Romans 5:3-4)

In the same way, the Spirit helps us in our weakness. We do not know what we ought to pray for, but the Spirit himself intercedes for us through wordless groans.
(Romans 8:26)

Spend some time experimenting with new ways to pray.

Be as creative as you like.

Here are two ideas you may not have tried before:

(During your session you may want to use the internet to explore further or you could print out some resources for each of the prayer ideas below. There is a lot of information available both online or in written books.)

Lectio Divina

The four steps to "Lectio Divina" are:

- Reading – choose a Bible verse or longer passage and read it.

- Meditating - spend some time thinking about the verse. Engage your senses, emotions and thinking as you absorb the words.

- Praying - take the parts of the verse that stood out to you and pray either with thanksgiving, petition, intercession or adoration. You might want to write down what you think God is saying to you through the verse.

- Now for the final part of Lectio Divina... (You can do this in a few minutes or you can take much longer.)

- Contemplating - reflect on what God is saying to you through this verse. Allow his presence to take the words you have written and move your heart to respond. Be aware of his presence.

Examen

There are so many different ways to use this method of prayer. You can take your time or it can be done fairly quickly. You can establish a morning prayer or a lunchtime prayer, you can adapt it for different times of the day.

Five easy steps:

1. Take some time to be aware of God's presence and invite the Holy Spirit to come.

2. Practise gratefulness. What are you thankful for? Actions, conversations, things you have seen around you, events that have happened

3. Take time to be aware of your emotions. We can often go through the day feeling things but never taking the time to be fully aware and fully present in the moment.

4. It's often as we stop and intentionally be fully present in the moment that we become aware of God's presence. Reflect on your thought and emotions of the day (or yesterday). Was there a moment God was speaking to you? Were there thoughts God wants you to be aware of now? Is there something he may be prompting you to do today?

5. Choose one thing you have been reminded of, or prompted to do or think about and spend some time in prayer with regard to it.

6. Allow some time to let hope arise for the future, today, tomorrow, next week or month or year. Allow God's presence to fill your thoughts, emotions and imagination.

If you have a smart phone you might consider downloading a prayer app to help you pray. For example;

Inner Room by 24-7 prayer app to help remind you when and what to pray. Or Sacred Space your daily prayer online app that helps you pray using a scripture each day.

 When I was young I learned to say my 'prayers'. As I got older I discovered an intimacy and immediacy in prayer that meant I abandoned my 'prayers'. As I've matured I've discovered again the strength of saying my 'prayers' - the ancient, crafted prayers that Christians have been saying for centuries - alongside my daily dialogue with Jesus.

Billy Kennedy

Over the edge

Prayer and fasting

To the delight of some and the annoyance of others, prayer and fasting pops up throughout God's word. Anna fasted in Luke, Cornelius and Paul in Acts. Jesus fasted for 40 days before beginning his public ministry.

Virtually all the great evangelists fasted and prayed. Charles Finney wrote in his autobiography that he had frequent days of prayer and fasting. John Wesley staunchly believed in fasting and personally fasted every Wednesday and Friday. Wesley gave much credit for the power and fruit of his ministry to the discipline of prayer and fasting. We don't fast to earn something, we fast for a connection with our supernatural God.

If you haven't fasted before why not commit some time to fast? It doesn't have to be from food. It may be that you choose to fast from watching TV or using your phone for a day or week.

If you have fasted before, how about developing a rhythm of fasting?

There are unlimited ways to pray and it seems there is always new ways to be discovered.

We can take comfort in knowing that however we pray when we pray to our father in heaven all of our prayers are precious. None are wasted as he regards them all as sweet smelling incense as they are gathered in golden bowls in heaven. Revelation 5: 3.

We have two teenage children and we love it when they want to talk to us about anything so how much more must God love it when we want to communicate with him.

He is looking forward to your prayer adventures yet to come.

Bonus creative prayer ideas

1. Look at an image or a photograph. Ask God what he wants to say about it. (You can do this with photographs of anything).

2. Feel an item – a stone, a small wooden cross, some soil, hands in water, leaves, seeds. Be present in the moment. Take time to experience God's presence as you touch or hold the item.

3. Pray through today's newspaper. Cut out particular stories of prayer interest.

4. Pray for every band you hear on the radio for an hour.

5. Sit in the supermarket car park and pray for everybody who goes by. Pray your best prayers over them.

6. Go on your local authority website, find the page with the councillors on and pray for each one; kingdom values, protection, comfort, bravery to stand up against injustice and wisdom.

7. Get your small group to meet to walk and pray around an area of your town.

8. Set your phone alarm to go off at hourly intervals with a message to remind you to pray.

9. Get some A4 paper and make some smart paper planes. Write all over them lots of prayer points and throw them up in the air calling out to God to answer the prayers on the plane.

10. At your small group play prayer musical chairs. Write different prayers on A4 paper, put on the seats, as the music stops, pray for the prayer request.

11. Buy a selection of culture magazines then cut out some stories and then take turns to share why you picked that feature and get everyone to pray into it.

12. Football prayers – pick a football team, roll two dice and match the squad number and pray for that player.

13. Grow sunflower seeds and at the end of the season harvest all the seeds and plant the seeds in strategic places and pray for God's sunshine to break into the darkness.

essential
christian

MAKING DISCIPLES

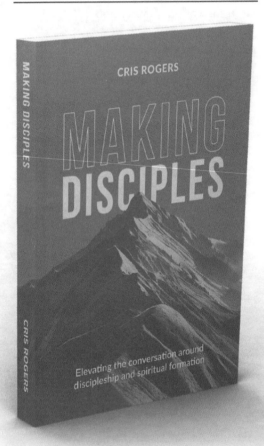

Jesus didn't tell his disciples to listen to him but to follow him
and see how he 'did' life in relationship with God.

Making Disciples is an assessment tool to be used by any church, small group or
individual interested in elevating the conversation around discipleship and spiritual
formation. Following an insightful seven-week course, this tool unpacks the user's
strengths and gifts and ultimately helps people grow and develop as disciples of Jesus.

Available at essentialchristian.org/store and Christian Bookshops

UNLIMITED:
A MANUAL FOR PRAYER

**Prayer is an adventure in which we explore a relationship.
It is not a set of problems to be navigated.**

This interactive book uses Jesus' teaching on prayer in Matthew 6
to help you pray. Pray for the first time, pray for the gazillionth time.
Pray in a new way or an old way, pray alone or with others. Just pray.

Your Online Christian Resource Store

Over **180,000** resources

Books | Music | Bibles | Song Scores
Teaching | DVDs | Church Supplies | Cards and Gifts

Shop online today at
essentialchristian.org/store